UndeR Wraps

written by Meish Goldish

SCHOLASTIC INC.

New York Toronto London Auckland Sydney
Mexico City New Delhi Hong Kong Buenos Aires

Developed by Kirchoff/Wohlberg, Inc., in cooperation with Scholastic Inc.
Credits appear on the inside back cover, which constitutes an extension of this copyright page.
Copyright © 2002 by Scholastic Inc.
All rights reserved. Published by Scholastic Inc. Printed in the U.S.A.
ISBN 0-439-35187-1
SCHOLASTIC and associated logos and designs are trademarks
and/or registered trademarks of Scholastic Inc.

3 4 5 6 7 8 9 10   23   09 08 07 06 05 04 03

What Is a Mummy?

You've probably seen a movie about mummies. Was it funny? Was it scary? Well, mummies are not monsters in bandages that chase people around. They have a long and fascinating history. Their story begins thousands of years ago in northern Africa, in the land of Egypt. The mummy of an Egyptian king was put in this beautiful mummy case before the king was buried.

The ancient Egyptians believed that death was followed by an afterlife in another world. They believed that a person would need his or her body in the next world. When a person died they thought it was important to preserve the person's body. It was especially important to preserve the body of a ruler. To preserve a body, the ancient Egyptians mummified it.

The body was wrapped in strips of thin linen cloth. The mummy was placed in a mummy case. Sometimes, a picture of the person was carved or painted on the outside of the case. The case was then put into a tomb. A king's tomb might have several rooms. Small figures of servants and objects that might be needed in the next world were buried along with the mummy.

The Mummy of King Tutankhamen

Most of the royal tombs were hidden for many, many years. Stories about the riches of the tombs were told, but most of these treasures were safely hidden from robbers.

Within the last century people discovered some of these tombs. One of the most famous discoveries was the tomb of King Tutankhamen.

Tutankhamen ruled in Egypt more than 3,000 years ago. He became a king when he was about nine years old. When he died at the age of eighteen, he was mummified. Then he was secretly put in his tomb. The tomb had four small rooms. They were filled with the things he would need in the next world. His tomb was located in an area called the Valley of the Kings.

Howard Carter was a British archeologist. He studied Egyptian tombs. After exploring in the Valley of the Kings for years, he discovered the tomb of King Tutankhamen in 1922. Imagine how excited people were when they heard the news!

When Carter entered the tomb, he was shocked to find that tomb robbers had been there before him. The tomb had been broken into twice, not long after the king's death. However, since that time, no one had entered it.

Then Carter found a sealed entrance to another room. He and his team broke through the wall. In the room, Carter found untouched treasures. He said that he had found "wonderful things!"

He saw four chariots. There were several gold-covered couches. There were chairs, royal robes, and musical instruments. He saw jewelry, bows and arrows, and dried foods. Carter and his crew worked to sort all the items.

Then they were ready to enter the burial room itself. A door was sealed into the wall and guarded by two life-sized statues. Carter broke through and peered into the room. He was dazzled by all the gleaming gold that he saw.

He found huge golden boxes nested one in another. Inside the last box was the mummy of King Tutankhamen. Covering the head and shoulders of the mummy was an amazing large, gold mask. Valuable jewels were set in the mask. Also in the room were beds, chairs, jewelry, and statues covered in gold.

More than 3,000 items were found in the four rooms. It took Carter and his team more than ten years to sort, photograph, and list the items. Among them were clothing, jewelry, swords, shields, ostrich feather fans, trumpets, animal figures, model ships, toys, games, and jars of precious oils.

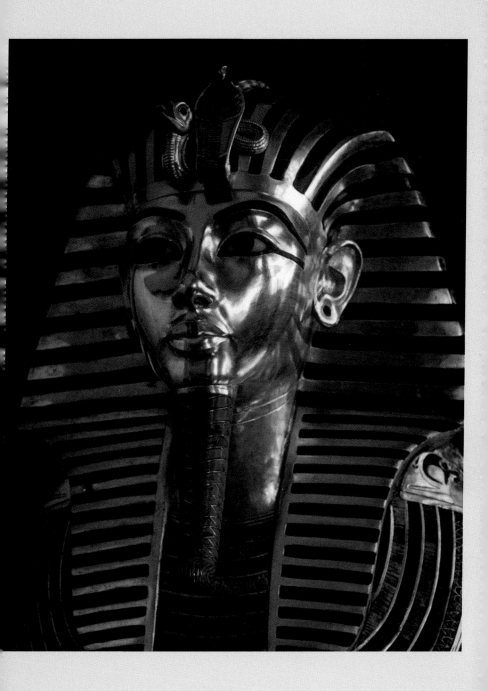

The items found in King Tutankhamen's tomb were made with great care. One piece was a beautiful throne. The king probably sat there when he met with his advisors. The throne was made of wood and covered with gold leaf. The surface of the gold was painted, in some places.

There is a lion's head at the end of each arm of the chair. The ancient Egyptians used lion heads on many pieces of furniture. Lion claws were carved on the legs of the chair. The arms of the chair are decorated with winged snakes. The ancient Egyptians believed that the snakes would protect the dead ruler from evil. On the next page, you can see the picture on the throne. It shows King Tutankhamen with his wife, Queen Ankhesenamun.

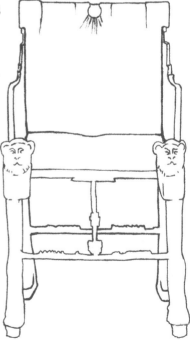

This king and queen were married when they were very young. After King Tutankhamen died, his wife remained queen for several years.

In the picture, it looks as if the king and queen are talking to each other. What do you think they might be saying?

The Mummy of Ramses the Great

About 50 years after the death of King Tutankhamen, Ramses II ruled in Egypt. Ramses the Great, as he is called, was a powerful king. He ruled Egypt for a long time.

During his rule, Ramses II began a large number of construction projects in Egypt. He had a new capital city built where the Nile River flows into the sea. He had a temple built at Karnak and another at Abu Simbel, where four gigantic stone statues of Ramses II guarded its entrance. Ramses the Great did not want to be forgotten. He wanted his images to be seen after he died. He was successful. We are still looking at his portraits in stone long after his sculptors carved and painted them.

During his reign, Ramses II traveled to where his projects were being built. After his death, his mummy traveled even further.

The original tomb for Ramses II was put in a secret place. Finding the burial place of a such a rich king was tempting. People knew he would be buried with gold and jewels. Robbers broke into the first tomb.

After the robbery, the mummy was moved to another tomb. Thieves broke in again. The mummy was moved again and again. Finally, the mummy was successfully hidden in rocky cliffs with other kings of ancient Egypt. The latest discovery was in modern times.

People all over the world have been fascinated with ancient Egyptian mummies and artifacts. Artists in ancient Egypt painted scenes that showed how people lived then, how they traveled, and what they wore. The pictures also showed animals that lived in ancient Egypt. The artists painted the walls of many tombs with scenes like these.

Many of the treasures taken out of royal tombs have been returned to Egypt. They can be seen in the Egyptian Museum in Cairo.

This picture shows the walls of the tomb of Queen Nefertari, the wife of Ramses II. You may recognize some of the figures shown here. For instance, do you see the bird on top of the archway that leads back into the tomb? That bird is a vulture. Vultures can be found all over the world today. If you look carefully, you may also see several other kinds of birds, a beetle, and some human figures. There are other figures here that you may not recognize. The ancient Egyptians knew who these figures were and what they meant.

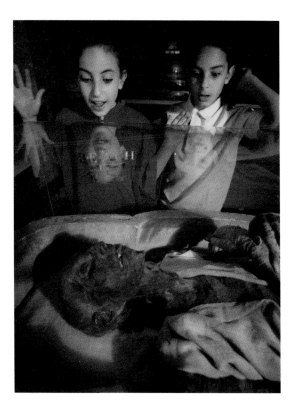

In 1976, a special exhibition was dedicated to Ramses II. The show's organizers wanted to display the ruler's mummy as well as his treasures. A great argument followed.

Should the mummy of Ramses II be put on display? Some archaeologists felt that the mummy was too fragile. Others argued that the body should be a part of the exhibit, no matter how fragile.

Today the mummy of Ramses II, like that of King Tutankhamen, can be seen in Egypt.